UP CLOSE

Sea Monsters

PAUL HARRISON

This paperback edition published in 2011 by Franklin Watts

Copyright © 2008 Arcturus Publishing Limited

Franklin Watts
338 Euston Road
London NW1 3BH

Franklin Watts Australia
Level 17/207 Kent Street
Sydney NSW 2000

Author: Paul Harrison
Designer (new edition): Silvie Rabbe
Editor (new edition): Fiona Tulloch

Picture credits: Bridgeman Art Library: page 2; Chris Harvey-Clark: page 13; Natural History Museum: page 5, top and bottom; Nature Picture Library: page 7, bottom; page 9, bottom; page 10; page 12, top and bottom; page 15;

Contents

What is a Sea

For centuries, sailors have come back from the sea with terrifying tales of mysterious creatures. Maybe the waves confuse the mind. Or perhaps there is some truth to these unlikely myths...

The biggest sea monsters are blue whales, which measure up to 38 metres long.

STRANGE WORLD

Many stories about sea monsters came from ships' passengers who didn't go to sea very often. If you saw a whale for the first time, you would probably think it was a monster too!

Monster?

SCARY

Exploring the seas was a spooky experience. Doing battle with stormy seas made explorers nervous. Travelling very far from home brought a fear of the unknown.

TERROR MAPS

Many old sea maps had pictures of monsters thought to be lurking in the depths. Sailors would plan their journeys around them.

The *carcasses* of strange sea creatures washed up on shore are called "globsters".

SCARE STORIES

Some early traders made up stories of sea monsters to scare other people away from the best trade routes.

MYSTERIOUS BONES

In the past, *superstition* was very common. Dinosaur fossils and strange bones found on beaches were believed to be evidence of dragons and sea monsters.

LURKING BENEATH

An octopus will eat almost anything. Its long *tentacles* are very strong and its suckers release chemicals which stun its prey.

NEW DISCOVERIES

New species of sea-dwellers are being discovered every day. In

discovered. It was over 6 metres long.

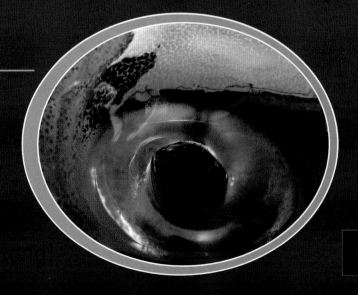

Ancient Monsters

Life developed in the sea long before it did on land. Some of the top predators on the planet used to live in the water. Here are some of the most impressive.

Sharks first appeared on earth around 400 million years ago.

SNAP!

The saltwater crocodile is the largest crocodile and grows to over 6 metres long. People used to think crocodiles were sea monsters.

TOOTHLESS TERROR

Over 360 million years ago, the *Dunkleosteus* (dun-klee-OS-tee-us) was bigger and scarier than today's great white shark.

MONSTROUS MAULER

The *Liopleurodon* (LIE-o-PLOOR-o-don) terrorized the seas 150 million years ago and grew up to 15 metres long.

NESSIE

Nessie is one of the most famous sea monsters and is believed to live in Loch Ness in Scotland. Nessie-spotters claim to have seen a long neck and a humped back gliding through the water.

Sea Serpents

The classic sea monster is the sea serpent. There have been reports of gigantic snake-like terrors in the oceans for many years.

INLAND SERPENTS

The most famous lake monsters are Nessie from Loch Ness, Ogopogo from Lake Okanagan in Canada, and Champ from Lake Champlain in the USA.

UNKNOWN TERROR

A large sea serpent nicknamed Chessie is said to live in Chesapeake Bay, USA. A videotape of the creature is too poor for scientists to say what Chessie really is.

In 1840, a ship's crew thought they'd seen a sea monster. It turned out to be a lump of seaweed!

ENORMOUS FISH

The oarfish is a kind of sea serpent that is around 9 metres long. Could this be the beast that sailors have been spotting for all these years?

FALSE IDENTITY

The anaconda, which lives in rivers, grows to over 9 metres long. Could these look like sea monsters?

Suckered In

Take a peek at a squid—it is one ugly creature! Their suckers and snake-like tentacles are enough to give most people nightmares.

Whales are often found with sucker marks on their skin from fights with giant squid.

THE MIGHTY KRAKEN

For many years there have been tales of the Kraken, a giant squid-like creature. People say it rises out of the sea and pulls boats under the waves.

Jules Verne
wrote about
sailors' stories of
monster attacks
in the book
*Twenty Thousand
Leagues Under
the Sea.*

GIANT OCTOPUS

The Lusca is a giant
octopus that is said to
live in the Caribbean.
Old photographs of a
body washed up on
shore suggest that it
might actually be real!

REAL-LIFE MONSTER

The closest living thing
to the Kraken is the giant
squid. These can grow up to
13 metres long. That's the
length of a bus!

13

Swallowed

Sailors had two main fears about being at sea: that their ship would sink, leaving them to drown, or that they would get eaten. But how likely is it that someone could get eaten at sea?

GENTLE GIANTS

There are many different types of whale, all of which grow very big. They are placid by nature—if they eat people, it's because people attack them first.

Whole

The throats of most sharks are too small to swallow a human.

BIG FISH

Basking sharks are the second biggest fish in the ocean but they are not aggressive creatures. They are sometimes called "sunfish".

JONAH'S TALE

The Bible says that Jonah was swallowed by a whale. He lived inside its belly for three days and three nights.

15

FATAL MISTAKE

Great white sharks sometimes eat people, but only because they think they are some kind of food.

LITTLE FOOD

Many whales look big enough to eat a person, but they actually eat tiny creatures called *krill*. They catch them using a comb-like bone in their mouths.

Deep sea Monsters

Not all sea monsters come from people's imaginations. There are many strange creatures in the ocean—especially at the very bottom.

FANG-TASTIC FISH

The viperfish has very scary teeth. They are so big that they can't even fit inside its mouth! Luckily, it is only 25 cm long.

The water pressure in the deep sea is like having 50 jumbo jets on top of you!

LURING THEM IN

Sunlight can't reach the bottom of the ocean, so sea creatures here have to create their own light.

AT THE BOTTOM

Only soft-bodied creatures such as jellyfish and sea anemones can withstand the pressure in deep waters.

BIG MOUTH

The gulper eel has a huge mouth that can unhinge to open very wide. It can then swallow prey as big as itself!

Up to 90 per cent of deep sea fish can produce their own light.

JEEPERS CREEPERS

The light in the Greenland shark's eyes is produced by a *parasite* that lives on its eyes. It is one of the largest sharks alive.

What Was That?

The only way to tell for sure whether there are sea monsters out there is to find them. The sea covers two thirds of the planet, so this is a very hard task.

"Cryptids" is what cryptozoologists call th monsters they look for.

SURPRISE

The megamouth shark was only discovered in 1976—when it was caught by chance! Some "monsters" may just be undiscovered species.

BEACHCOMBING

Sometimes scientists don't have to go looking for new creatures. The sea washes up many interesting creatures, or fishermen catch them by mistake.

CRAZY OR CLEVER?

Looking for animals that most people believe are extinct or mythical is called "cryptozoology".

HIDE AND SEEK

Most of the sea remains unexplored. The sea bed provides plenty of places for creatures to hide in.

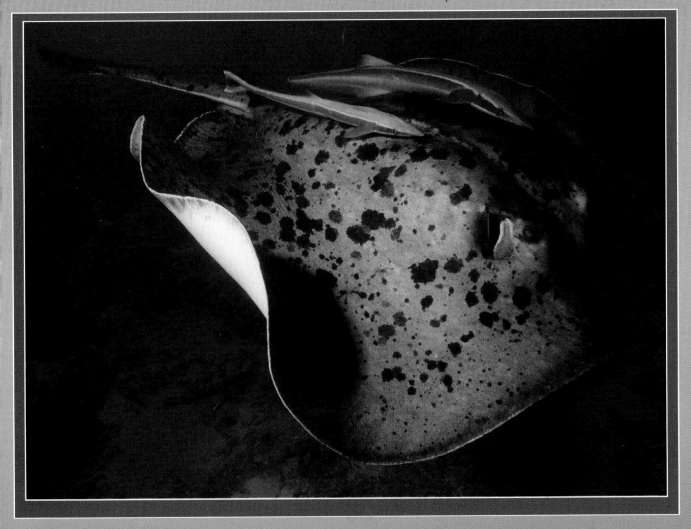

Glossary

CARCASS
The dead body of an animal.

DUNKLEOSTEUS
An enormous prehistoric fish which is now extinct.

KRILL
Small shrimp-like sea creatures that many bigger fish eat.

LIOPLEURODON
A very large prehistoric fish from around 150 million years ago.

PARASITE
An organism that lives on an animal or plant but doesn't help it survive.

SUPERSTITION
An unproven belief that actions or events are caused by supernatural forces.

TENTACLES
Flexible feelers some animals have instead of arms and legs. They are used for grasping, moving about, sensing touch, cold, etc.

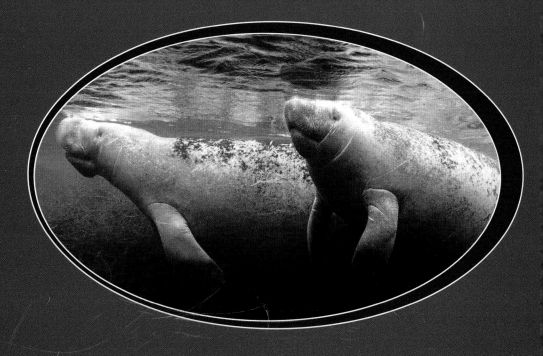

Further Reading

Chased by Sea Monsters: Prehistoric Predators of the Deep
Nigel Marven and Jasper James,
DK, 2003

Enclyclopedia Prehistorica: Sharks and Other Sea Monsters
Robert Sabuda and Matthew Reinhart,
Candlewick Press, 2006

Sea Monsters
Dr Stephen Cumbaa, Kids Can Press, 2007

Sea Monsters
Aaron Sautter, Coughlan Publishing, 2006

The Book of Sea Monsters
Nigel Suckling and Bob Eggleton,
Paper Tiger Books, 1998

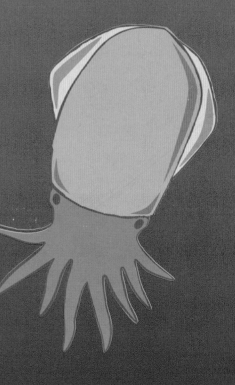

Index